Down to my I

Poems

Antjie Krog

RANDOM
POETS

First published in South Africa in 2000 by
Random House (Pty) Ltd
Endulini, 5a Jubilee Road, Parktown 2193
Johannesburg, South Africa
Reg. No. 66/03153/07

Postal address: P.O. Box 2263, Parklands 2121
South Africa

First published 2000
Second impression 2003

Produced for Random House by
Francolin Publishers (Pty) Ltd, Cape Town

Project manager: Douglas van der Horst
Design and layout: Sarah-Anne Raynham
Cover design: Sarah-Anne Raynham

Illustrations of *Themeda triandra* by Maré Liebenberg

Reproduction by Image Mix
Printing and binding by CTP Book Printers,
Duminy Street, Parow 7500, Cape Town, South Africa

ISBN 0-9584195-5-8

NOTES

OVER the years several people have translated various poems of mine into English. Initially this was quite a disturbing experience: I felt alienated from the translations, which seemed too English and remote from their Afrikaans origins. At the same time, however, I longed to interact as a poet with South Africans who do not read Afrikaans – in the same way that I was communicating with an enthusiastic Afrikaans audience. I often had to translate my poems for black students or for poets with whom I shared a stage at rallies and poetry readings. But how can one communicate, other than in a fragmented way, when poems have been translated at random based on the personal choices of others?

When I started working on *Country of My Skull* I found a kind of solution: I wrote the text in Afrikaans and translated it myself into English, keeping the underlying Afrikaans structure and rhythm intact. In this way I came to feel completely integrated with the book.

The biggest loss in translated poetry is the sound of the original language, a key element that completely disappears when a work is translated into an unrelated language. Afrikaans into Dutch, for example, captures much more of the original sound than Afrikaans into English or Zulu. The translator of poetry has several choices: either to stay as close as possible to the meaning of the original poem, hoping that the translation will create its own internal rhythm; or to search for equally rich sounds and rhythms in the language of the translation and risk introducing new resonances of meaning; or to create a 'version' of the original that is in many respects a new poem.

Although I exercised all these choices, I still experienced problems.

Some of the poems, like the Susanna Smit series with its clipped or ecstatic language, didn't work at all and had to be abandoned. It was also impossible to recapture the tight thematic and stylistic structure of a volume like *Jerusalemgangers*, which had haplography as both its central theme and style, or the complexity of the devices used to produce a political text in the process of disrupting itself, as occurs in *Lady Anne*.

Also lost in the translations of my poems is the echo of other

Afrikaans poets and the ways in which I have used their well-known works – for example the close relationship between the calm, beautiful motherhood verse of Elisabeth Eybers and my loud, noisy household poems; the traces of the first Afrikaans poems; and the response of my poems to the male voices of Van Wyk Louw, Opperman and Breytenbach.

Another complication is the different forms of spoken Afrikaans – so laden with power relationships, memory and longing – which are impossible to reproduce in another language. The context of political agony, repression, anger, violence and fear in which most of these poems were originally written is also very difficult to capture.

Literature is constantly retranslated for new eras. In the case of some of the earlier poems I tried to recreate the newness of then, but also took the liberty of exploring the same theme from a later perspective.

Some of my favourite translations by other poets are included in this volume. However, this selection would not have settled in the way it has without the help of P.S. Prabhakara, who corrected the grammar of the first draft, or without the sensitive, intelligent and professional care of fellow poet Karen Press. With open-minded glee she turned the somewhat congested manuscript into an adventure. She is one who truly reads with her tongue!

A.K.

Publisher's Note

RANDOM HOUSE first published Antjie Krog's *Country of My Skull* in South Africa in April 1998. It met with widespread acclaim and received several major prizes at home and upon publication in markets abroad. Remarkably, *Country of My Skull* was this writer's first prose work originally published in English.

Krog's poetry in Afrikaans, however, had pervaded South Africa for thirty years before the publication of *Country of My Skull*. Her poems were included in prescribed anthologies, essential material for the study of Afrikaans at school, an obligatory subject for every South African child, regardless of its mother tongue, until only a few years ago.

Born into a family of writers in 1952 on the farm Middenspruit in the Kroonstad district of the Free State province, Krog won her first national prize for writing when she was ten years old. At the age of seventeen and in her penultimate year at school, several of her poems and an essay were awarded a Gold Diploma at the local eisteddfod. These were included in a special edition of the school's annual magazine and their explicit political and sexual themes provoked such an angry response from certain sectors of the Kroonstad community that the controversy was highlighted in the country's national Afrikaans Sunday newspaper. The poem 'My Mooi Land' as well as some erotic passages from the essay were splashed across two pages of the newspaper along with rigorous comment, largely condemnatory, from a range of people.

One counterpoint to this mêlée was the mountain of letters of support from mainly black scholars posted to Krog's school. Several months later, the Sunday paper that had started it all published news of the translation of 'My Mooi Land' into English, and, worse still, of its publication in the ANC's mouthpiece in Dar es Salaam.

Such heresy demanded action in those dismal days and a publisher asked to see everything that Krog had written so that the famous Afrikaans poet D.J. Opperman could determine whether or not Krog possessed any real talent. Contrary to the prevailing expectations, Opperman recommended publication and Krog's first volume of poetry, *Dogter van Jefta*, was published two weeks before her eighteenth birthday, without, though, the offending poem, 'My Mooi Land'.

Eight volumes of Krog's poems have been published since then and she has won most of the major literary prizes available in Afrikaans, including the esteemed Hertzog Prize for her volume entitled *Lady Anne* as well as the Dutch/Flemish Prize, the Reina Prinsen Geerling award. Krog has also published two volumes of poetry for children in Afrikaans as well as the novella *Relaas van 'n Moord* which was translated into English as *Account of a Murder* by Karen Press, a valued co-worker on this collection.

Although 'My Mooi Land' disappeared from Krog's oeuvre in South Africa, the poem lived a telling life of its own after the stir it had initially caused. When the first political prisoners were released from Robben Island, Ahmed Kathrada read it to an audience of thousands at a mass rally in Soweto at the end of October 1989, mentioning the hope that the words of an Afrikaans child had instilled among those held captive on the island.

Although collections of Krog's poems have appeared in Dutch and French translations, *Down to My Last Skin* is the first to be published in the English language.

Parktown, Johannesburg
July 2000

CONTENTS

One
First poems

my beautiful land

look, I build myself a land
where skin colour doesn't count
only the inner brand of self

where no goat face in parliament
can keep things permanently verkramp

where I can love you,
can lie beside you in the grass
without saying "I do"

where we sing with guitars at night
where we bring gifts of white jasmine

where I don't have to poison you
when foreign doves coo in my hair

where no court of law
will deaden the eyes of my children

where black and white hand in hand
can bring peace and love
in my beautiful land

(1969)

ma

ma I am writing a poem for you
without fancy punctuation
without words that rhyme
without adjectives
just sommer
a barefoot poem –

because you raise me
in your small halting hands
you chisel me with your black eyes
and pointed words
you turn your slate head
you laugh and collapse my tents
but every night you offer me
to your Lord God
your mole-marked ear is my only telephone
your house my only bible
your name my breakwater against life

I am so sorry ma
that I am not
what I so much want to be for you

(1969)

(translated by Karen Press)

daughter of Jephthah

Lord at the Plain of the Vineyards
Lord at Mizpeh in Gilead
Lord God of Jephthah
here is my body!
here is my hymen – safe as a retina
        and whole as a green pomegranate
here is my abdomen – a cold fireplace
        that will watch resigned over the monthly flow
here are my breasts – two bleeding drops
        that will never be leavened with love
here are my hands dear Lord
        strong and willing as my heart
from now on I am Your bride
        impregnated with spirit
from now on I am midwife to a nation
from now on I expect
You

(1970)

outside nineveh

somewhere close to nineveh there is a tree:
a small tree with separate white thorns
    with a small europe
    in its africa

those who sit in your shade don't sing to you
those who reap your seeds never give you water
and they cheer the worm in your trunk
they celebrate your sickle eyes
they celebrate the paws that keep on walking
    keep on keep on walking

I will make a song for you, my little tree
I will pray for you
because wherever I sleep at night
I stay your thorn
I stay white

(1970)

maths

every day I die for 35 minutes
tangented at my desk
a crow caws in front of the class
feeding me maths

to prove: Draw line AB and then find C
proof: I draw AB
               I construct a perpendicular
               up ... past the stars
               and find C
               alone
               on Pythagoras he sits cross-legged
               howling
               so bloody bloody
               bloody lonely

(1969)

biology class

yell
push
past the desks to the front
surround the table
lens in hand
shut up frantically to hear the din

suddenly she stands in the door: a white dove
vulnerable between the leaves of her palms

push to the inside
strain
shout:
slaughter him, slaughter him
we have to pass standard nine
splint his body on a plank
explain class aves
take scissors
snip him open
the tiny heart in her fingers
she laughs
her bloody hands

suddenly I see through my lens
his neck draped like an altar tassel
which is the precise moment his Eyes
move into mine

(1969)

16

sonnet (tonight)

tonight I know
that I will never love you again:

your hands have become too small
to hold me
your body too slender
to release me

I flooded loose from pain and sadness
and from you
I saw cows rising from the grass
I saw a day dying like a bird on its back

I have to get up
I have to break a horizon
because I am tired
of your wet snout in my thigh

(1971)

University of the Orange Free State

and suddenly I stand alone
just   completely
alone
a windmill among shoulders
with daybreak – slowly and bloody –
directions of wind are born:

my beautiful north
throws open a dassie rug of soft free state
our home glides downslope like a die
through the red grass that trots sniffling down the rain

from the south a sun peals with laughter
through everything which once was beautiful to me
shattering all I once held true

in the west the sky laments   a big blue tuba
and a bird loosens itself from the spout
ill with inflammation and freedom

the east jumps open like a suitcase lid
and all borders recoil before the procession
building steps around the earth

and among all the wind and trees and sun
I begin to look for the small switch of my   origin

(1971)

Two

Love is all i know

the day surrenders to its sadness

the day surrenders to its sadness
over palm tree and roof the rain reigns mercilessly
the small white house with trellis and high verandah
stands like a warm cow her backside to the rain
eyes tightly shut

inside a woman moves from window to window
as beautiful as sunlight through vine leaves
as beautiful the drops on green
the rain on avocado bark
on the flintstone of leaves
the bougainvillaea sparkling wet, sly
keel green of apricots

the double hibiscus groans desperate and red in the dark

the intimacy inside is tangible
children sleeping damp in their room
the man in front of the heater
with art book cigarette and wine   his eyes
glance up somewhat drenched in love

dusk snuffles softly against the gutters
a woman wanders from one steamed window to another
and sees the house constantly from an outside perspective
disabled and thanks to the light in every window
barely conscious of the total magnitude

a warm cow her backside to the rain

ode to a perfect match

on this Monday morning
on which Mavis didn't turn up
amongst washing and toys
in my bra and panties on the carpet
John Lennon through the speakers
   oh my lover for the first time in my life
   my eyes can see
your children busy fighting
I let my hair frizz out
throw the door open against the green
abandon the housekeeping

to write you an ode

where you sit behind your drawing board
eyes narrowed behind a dunhill spiral
with the isometric projection of St Paul's Cathedral
and a nursery school drawing on the wall
   divorces don't surprise you you said last night
   because one in a hundred finds a perfect match
that I love you is an understatement
that I cannot live without you a cliché
between our fights our children our stuttering household
the boredom of translations and public latrines
we are a miraculously perfect match

tonight when I press my breasts against you
my wrists gliding over your thick shining hair
when I rotate around your eyes
(after all these years still acrimoniously blue)
this Monday pastoral says
that our love is all I know
and all I need to know

salad

with a sharp knife
I shred the hairless tomato
the wrinkled parsley
and the onion-round navel
the cucumber crunches fresh under the carving blade
mixed with salt, pepper, saliva and oil
stirred with semen mayonnaise
I serve it
in the smooth cool lettuce of your thighs

with a smile you get up
pour dark wine into every glass
mercy is absent in your napkin-blue eyes
razor sharp your toast to us

after the first mouthful
I excuse myself from the table
flee to the bathroom
and chew my knuckles
to bone china

the children show us

the children show us a wedding photograph
see how funny Dad looks
with the photo in my hand
my whole body dulls with pain

oh my most beloved love
man that once was whole
with hair so luxuriously buoyantly dark
your face so slender so arrogant
your nostrils despise the spectacle of photographer
a waistcoat frames your broad chest
your grey woollen jacket tilts carelessly over your shoulder
your right arm my husband
curls lightly around my waist
the palm half open towards my breast
your eyes glitter haughty with impatience
for the honeymoon now

with your battered bride

I don't glance at your grizzled hair

I don't glance at your grizzled hair
the tarnishing of fingers and teeth
first signs of plumpness at belly and rib
I hear only how your voice holds sway
a house around me keeping elements at bay

I no longer glance at your weary eyes
but I watch your hands
weigh up child after child
and lay out our makeshift strategies

you endure me
you define me
you prop me on my feet
you fuse my explosive energies
sardonically weld masks for my chest

I make you
middle-aged

oh hold me have me
overcome now kiss me
your moustache combing through my marrow
(not the man to master his woman
by way of some erotic web)
only tell me you take me
desire desire again
desire once again fire
my body till it seems I strangely vibrate
swell into my awkward defenceless breadwinner
uncork that fragrance careening and young
again be   come   we'll be again
all day all night long cock-full of fun

(translated by Denis Hirson)

sonnet (I will always remember)

I will always remember the way you walked
in last night – you moved as if sparks
flew from you your eyes a mean
messy blue   then you held me as always

so that I had to raise my eyes up to your secure mouth
your face determined your hands your neck your shoulders
cut under the impeccable shirt I smelled
on you the perfume of power   as your dark head

bent down to greet every child something
authoritarian stayed with your body as of one
who always lies on top your hands moved
with the orders of a boss   this morning I bring

breakfast – on the bedside table you put my monthly allowance –
and I see how the word finance also breathes the word violence

illness

the August wind dusts down the street
where I wait for the children in the car
a disconsolate haze hangs over the suburb
low dust fleeces the grass and fluttering daisies
I think of you on a high hospital bed
you have been for so long with me against me of me
I try to imagine you
loose   ·
someone apart from me away from me from us
with difficulty I get you standing apart
loose and with the looseness
a fragility
as you must lie there
slender in your loosely striped pyjamas
and I think about how you are being overcome
more and more by this marriage
how surely the weight of it
burdens your thin wrists
how your heart − treacherous from stress −
like a tilting bird swerves behind your ribs

I think of your eyes when you greeted me
how like death they retreated how dry your tongue
how purulent the blister on your lip
what has become of you who are mine − suddenly
the bell and our children
rearing against the wind so pale
so inclined towards each other so frail
so apart as if wind is all they know
you are all we have you know
that holds us against each other as if related

and I think of you
as of blood I think of you
while we drive on in silence
through this endless dismal August day

latin-american love song

neither the moist intimacy of your eyelids   fair as fennel
nor the violence of your body withholding behind sheets
nor what comes to me as your life
will have so much slender mercy for me
as to see you sleeping

perhaps I see you sometimes
for the first time

you with your chest of guava and grape
your hands cool as spoons
your haughty griefs stain every corner blue

we will endure with each other

even if the sun culls the rooftops
even if the state cooks clichés
we will fill our hearts with colour
and the fireworks of finches
even if my eyes ride a rag to the horizon
even if the moon comes bareback
even if the mountain forms a conspiracy against the night

we will persist with each other
sometimes I see you for the first time

my words of love

my words of love grow more tenuous than the sound of lilac
my language frayed
dazed and softened I feel myself through your stubborn struggle

you still hold me close like no one else
you still choose my side like no one else
against your chest I lie and I confess
you hunt my every gesture
you catch up with me everywhere
you pull me down between bush and grass
on the footpath you turn me around
        so that I must look you in the eye
you kick me in the balls
you shake me by the skin of my neck
you hold me, prick in the back, on the straight and narrow

(translated by Karen Press)

marital psalm

this marriage is my shepherd
I shall not want
in a swoon he loves me
and lusts after me with disconcerting fitness
man who makes me possible
(though I can fight him spectacularly)
(the way we make a double bed
shows an undivided indestructible pact)

sometimes he catches me by the hind leg
as one big piece of solid treachery
persecutes me
fucks me day and night
violates every millimetre of private space
smothers every glint in my eye which could lead to writing

"do our children successfully in respectable schools have to see
how their friends read about their mother's splashing cunt
and their father's perished cock
I mean my wife
jesus! somewhere a man's got to draw the line"

I will fear no evil
the rod and the staff they comfort me

stripping

while you undress
I watch through my lashes
that bloody thick cock
prudish and self-righteous it hangs
head neatly wrinkled and clear cut
about its place between the balls – wincing in my direction

and I think of its years and years of conquest
night after fucking night through pregnancies
menstruation abortion pill-indifference
sorrow how many lectures given honours
received shopping done with semen dripping
on the everyday pad from all sides
that blade cuts

that cock goddamit does more than conquer
it determines how generous the mood
how matter-of-fact how daring the expenditure
standing upright it is bend or open-up
and you better be impressed my sister
not merely lushy or horny
but in bloody awe, yes!
everything every godfucking thing revolves around the maintenance
of cock
and the thing has no heart no brain no soul
it's dictatorial a fat-lipped autocrat
a mister's Mister

somewhere you note numbers and statistics
that morning in Paris and again that night
your hands full of tit

I am waiting for the day
oh I look forward to the day the cock crumbles
that it doesn't want to
that in a rosepoint pout it swings only hither and dither
that it doesn't ever want to flare
but wiggle waggles unwillingly
boils over like a jam pot or fritters away like a balloon

and come it will come
because rumour has it
that for generations
the women in my family kapater their men with
yes with stares
oh jesus, and then we slither away like fertile snakes in the grass
taking shit from nobody
and they tell me
my aunts and my nieces and sisters they laugh and tell me
how one's body starts chatting then how it dances into tune
at last coming home to its own juices

THREE
DEAR CHILD OF THE LEAN FLANK

first sign of life

you moved in me today
perhaps you turned
or adjusted a limb in the dark
you were not urgent
nor rowdy
just inescapably here
with my hand across my abdomen
I wanted to hold you in words
how you look
how you sound
how I am going to utter you
but you drifted wordlessly in placenta

like a poem you began without my knowing
a coupling of image and sound
with an umbilical cord to life veined through my blood
after weeks swollen into a gesture of word and vertebrae
a verse trembling this morning into wanting to be written

caught in a tender vortex of sun
my hairbrush forgotten in my hand
I was suddenly utterly lonely in astonishment
about this omen
of a yet unwritten, but most awe-inspiring poem

birth

at last this lovely little mammoth godawful in roses and blood
straining lovely between my legs tore loose
tumbled, no slipped out besmeared into my arms yelling birth
yelling pain yelling strength oh I throb throb throb about my
boychild my onlyest my loveliest my smallest my most superlative
sound
wash him with colostrum
his arms next to his body wrap him in nappies
in a manger of songs shy murmurs from a twilight room
and feed him
feed him oh free feed him from my heart

how and with what?

I dig rennets from the sink sieve
oats and rinds burp into the drain outside the window
the nappy liners are being stunk out into the toilet
the dirty nappies sunlight soaped
bottoms washed powdered
the one cries with hunger
the other with anger
the eldest with his nervous vegetable knife voice
carves a whole superman flight through the noise
my man closes the door against us all
and turns up the Mozart piano concerto

and I go crazy

my voice yells a mixerpulpershreddermincer
my nose leaks like a fridge
my eyes quake like eggs in boiling water
my ears are post boxes pouting with calendars and junk mail
my children assault me with their rowdiness
    selfishness
    cheekiness
    destructiveness
their fears complexes insecurities threats needs
    beat my "image as mother" into soft steak on the wooden floor
I smell of vomit and shit and sweat
    of semen and leeks
I illustrate a kitchen
    with hair whipping dull against novilon skin
    the milk coupons of my back bent uninterestedly inside the gown
    the legs veined like blue soap
    slippers like pot scourers
I sulk like a flour bag
I am chipped like a jug
my hands drier and older than yesterday's toast
give half-hearted slaps against the clamour

I go outside and sit on the step this Sunday morning
neither sober nor embarrassed
wondering

how and with what does one survive this?

family figures as poetry material

from behind my desk through the burglar bars
I see the threesome walking home

the youngest: ragdoll-droophead-blue-eyed one
hair in the air like carrot tops
his little arms harvest cheerful redcheek noise

my daughter: mommy-dearest-bodily body
with dress skip walk and delighted little yells
dance-dances down her own songlet

my eldest: drags his red fire brigade boots
with his spindly legs   fights
with his chapped little fists against the air

my heart folds in my breast
why do they already look so desolate so apart?
what kinds of strange toys
will they soon be maimed into?

my stooping husband opens the gate for them,
cigarette in hand

the pen clatters from my hand
displays verses two, three, four and six
through my own illegible handwriting
into a public mix

second birthday

this morning when you burst into our room
    with balloons and whistles
    with presents in string
    your eyes assessing us warm as sleep

when you laughingly chased us
with your water pistol from the bed

I wondered:
what this morning is your other father doing?

transparency of the sole

the light over my desk
streams into darkness
I await my visitors on paper

my four children
finely balanced between anal and dorsal
tiny fins at the throat constantly stirring
eyes uncommonly soft
in the shallow brackish water your mother treads clay
with metaphors

come here across dictionaries and blank pages
how I love this delicate little school
these fish of mine in their four-strong flotilla
lure so close now what should I feed you?

dear child of the lean flank
yield to the seabed
yes the stretching makes you
ache but mother holds you to her mother
is here

the lower eye like father's wondrous blue
migrates cautiously with a complex bunching
of nerve and muscle
till it's up beside the other
pert little mouth almost pulled out of shape
with time the tongue will settle in its groove
pigment of the upper flank beginning to darken

unobtrusive between sand and stone you lie
meshed with bedrock never
again to prey or take flight
I press my mouth against each distended face mother knows

you will survive the tide

(translated by Denis Hirson)

for my daughter

full of foreboding I sit
sewing name tags
on clothes from which she gleams like sheen through my fingers
her hard shins
and white-gnarled high calcaneus bone
as she walks among other girls

this child holds to me
embraces   shows herself off to me
and I sit   sit sticklike
revolted
and flattered

an unaccustomedness I want in her
resistance   stand against   turn the back
against the surrender of an enticing body
rather reel from self-confidence my daughter
sharpen your blue dangling eyes
trust the lash of your thick platinum plait

resist my understanding
see my own unliberation
my inadequate sinewy heart
my entrapment
and the absolute fake that I am
acknowledge the chill around me

on the other hand
do not even bother with this poem
from your well-known mother
let it wash down your back
soft   trusting
as you are lying reading on your bed now
you already need no menace
to be so   more
than me

for my son

the earth hangs unfinished
and when the wind starts
the child stands in Kloof Street with his school bag

child of mine! I call to his back
there where my heart is tightest

as always I am elsewhere
I think him into almonds
and arms full of pulled up light
I trace his whispers in my matrix of blood

shyly the child shoots across the street
the wind takes his orthodontic drool

it is me
            your mother
but his eyes are on the brink of leaving me
the earth lies unfinished
the wind splinters from him all that is child
and I tighten about him
past guilt past all neglect

I love him
way
way beyond heart

ma will be late

that I come back to you
tired and without memory
that the kitchen door is open I

shuffle in with suitcases hurriedly bought presents
my family's distressed dreams
slink down the corridor the windows stained

with their abandoned language in the hard
bathroom light I brush my teeth
put a pill on my tongue: Thur

that I walk past where my daughter sleeps
her sheet neatly folded beneath her chin
on the dressing table silkworms rear in gold

that I can pass my sons
frowning like fists against their pillows
their restless undertones bruise the room

that I can rummage a nightie from the drawer
slip into the dark slit behind your back
that the warmth flows across to me

makes me neither poet nor human
in the ambush of breath
I die into woman

extenuating circumstances

every word stubbornly tilted into writing
betrays the lunacy
lying just below the vocal cords

all the more strangely it leaks

down the jugular
molars shredding mouthlinings
the breast silts up with something that could be pain

I stretch my hands: come
come graphite! come paper! come language!
come to my sanity
and bring mildness afterwards

in the tidy sitting room on the couch
the youngest skew on his dad's chest
sits my whole family
beheaded
with aortas reeling staining
through the spittlesoft sounds
the blubbering blood swabs
I recognise fragments of clothing
and the third child's turned-in fourth toe

under my nails grass splints

FOUR
TO BREATHE

nightmare of A Samuel born Krog

the desk is warm and bloody like a newly slaughtered carcass
from the drawers transparent synovial fluid drips
the chair against my back becomes big and pulpy
knocks and croaks like a frog
the clothes on my body take on a life of their own
they rear like snakes and breathe like fish
my tongue jumps around tail upright acrimonious
the salivary glands rattle their pincers
my hand falls on the white breath of the page
an animal with fur on its back
the pen becomes a soft hairy nicotine-stained finger
the letters it writes listlessly start decomposing at once
books swell with indignation
the typewriter grinds its olivetti teeth

I write because I am furious

poem making

something finely done:
it might be a poem
I make this morning

joy at once upon me
that falls looselimbed
about my desk, as though
wings at once were wrapped
around me   fresh
feathers crackling

nobody gets at me:
I think   I gaze
with double vision through
my fine cool house
and through it flows
Lamento di Federico
and into the garden
of flowers and birds

I bathe in the words
inhabit once more my body
hug my family, love them
and never become
one part of them: their needs
and dreams don't touch me

I play the game with words:
escape   arrange
tie up   jump free
collude   cheat and destroy
for nothing
a poem makes you free

I stick my hand
right into the blaze
that glows around me
softly lightly

and the phone rings for a children's party

the children attack me
like goats and I kiss them
cuddle them   over the huge
outstretching fields of maize
a sparrow hawk tumbles
playing among the flying ants
that burn like angels

(translated by Patrick Cullinan)

two years this month

two years this month
since my last volume of poetry
two years without a single line – dark

without even a thought that may lead to a poem

this is the way I want my life this
binding of an unwritten house: every child
ironed, folded, handed over warm and useable
so I say and so I pencil
around my ruins bleak and
misplaced shying away

suspend all correspondence translation
analysis and come to sit
before the clean page

how does one start a poem?

sharp turkish red pencil fragrant rubber
I split my ears inward
tap against the inner sides to intercept tremors
desperately I flog every wound

but inside it stays prudently thickened

... for some reason an opening suddenly pouts
something vibrates, my breath tones down

into a restrained shiver I wait
point of the pencil hovers   ah

the pulse of the fabric is emerging
my senses bunch lightly against one another

a child calls from afar / a door slams / footsteps down the passage

I grab the opening – please even a spurt will do
urgently cradle the closing muscle

but death starts at my feet I am
standing before a closed slippery inside

carefully the child enters the room / mom are you busy? /
his eyes ragged and grey

toilet poem

things of course about which one would never write a poem
force their way into the territory of poetic themes
such as changing tampon and pad to pee in toilets
of townships where one comes

on the floor water and effluent almost ankle deep
I wade on adidas soles like a cat

no moveable equipment available
like toilet seats bins hooks locks doors

my jacket hangs around my neck in blanket folds
handbag clutched between teeth

tampon – swollen red mouse, stained pad
wrapped in bank counterfoils

I piss shuddering rigid half squatting
between my legs

into a toilet bowl heaped halfway up
with at least four different colours of shit

every nerve ending erect with revulsion, poised to go mad
if just one drop should splash against me

(translated by Karen Press)

parole

I feel I lie because I blatantly indulge
in words
and useless eras
in the face of so much injustice
if poetry perseveres as luxury it also becomes a lie

I live on the other side of injustice
therefore I have the time
to tune chords precisely around the private gland
and why not? this country
has already been ruined

>   the order comes: words should be AK47s
>   should always fight   poetry should be useable
>   deed   relate the struggle   take sides
>   weeds are mightier than roses
>   tortured poetry grows wild in phonetic rain

(how can I safeguard
this poem against the stupidity
of politics? distressed
I stand, looked upon with suspicion,
my most ordinary words refused)

>   I am shamed by the poet's unheard of poetry
>   which screams on the other side of all breath
>   there where your eyes stop now: gravel road
>   spaza someone may have disappeared
>   before dawn; the wind moves as if in war
>   children kick a ball in the townships where three quarters

of the world lives and waits rightly so
on equality   shy like you   brave
or stupid or perhaps already lazy and corrupt like
us   from their hands hangs this treacherous carpet
of hope and hunger and dream

but the poet stands aside
he hears of petitions
motions of injustice
he has stopped writing poems
no poetry
the thoughtful poet stands smokeblue with cold

barely audible
she repeats her arrest
her sentence
melts from her tongue
not in print
not in photographs
not in statistics
everywhere it is damp
rumours of disappearances
torture
and anonymous deaths

the struggle filters
through with inaudible fierce noises
into the shady
suburbs
this has become a country of rumours

if my senses
cannot wean the cries from the leaves
or the blood from the barricades of groceries
or pick up murder from the blockades near to my desk
I will die hardened
in the crossfire of pencil and paper
which always fight back to the truth
>
> all the writers are dead aren't they
> they can't write "about" or "of" the oppressed
> and the oppressed writer is drowning in anger
> − this is what's being said
>
> "aesthetics is the only ethic"
> they say as well
> but the demands do not tolerate neutral ground

between two evils I chose neither

I was born
from a guild
of greed and scorn
where I always felt myself apart

a hedge between myself
and them   myself and the slaughter

nothing ever prepared me for hunger and homelessness
landlessness   I try to find a bridge
but everything is burning and I am looking for a guide

beware of propaganda   rhetoric
coarse chains of words under the whip of lies
without even the charm of consciousness
is aesthetics ever useful?

I never stop
studying
survival
with this fragile most light-hearted category
I investigate diligently every relation
to breathe to breathe yes to breathe
language has never been useless or fake

but only   although the poet may desire indulgence
and the progression of political words
the injustice is real
and whatever I write which will survive
sprouts from the feudal clash between lyddite and lie

(after reading Carolyn Forché and Stephen Watson)

poet becoming

to awake one morning into sound
with the antennae of vowel and consonant and diphthong
to calibrate with delicate care the subtlest
movement of light and loss in sound

to find yourself suddenly kneeling at the audible
palpable outline of a word – searching
for that precise moment in which
a poetic line expands in air

when the meaning of a word yields, slips
and then surrenders into tone – from then
the blood yearns for that infinite pitch of a word
because: the only truth stands skinned in sound

the poet writes poetry with her tongue
yes, she breathes deeply with her ear

FIVE
LADY ANNE

Lady Anne Barnard at the Cape

(a)
villanelle for the cape of good hope
Castle April 1798

they cling transparent ochre to stone and rusted ironwrought
leaves of Capse Rose and Rosa Odorata flourish in the fountain
from the Peacock room a strange light cleaves the inner court

since our arrival this spot has shuddered in my brain
out of autumn gossamer the sun produced a splendid snare
leaves of Capse Rose and Rosa Odorata flourish in the fountain

in each draft the light rambles towards you but nought
captures your cape the allure of your neck slightly turned
from the Peacock room a strange light cleaves the inner court

brittle alabaster your axils where sprigs sprout in textures of tin
threads of woven southern light taken in tow
leaves of Capse Rose and Rosa Odorata flourish in the fountain

oh it's only paradise I sought where the sun lords
and drifts towards us in fluent glory of sea and mountain blue
from the Peacock room a strange light cleaves the inner court

beloved   I have uncovered a continent for us thus bought
by famous apostles to contain all our hesitant ecstasies
leaves of Capse Rose and Rosa Odorata flourish in the fountain
from the Peacock room a strange light cleaves the inner court

(translated by Ada Serfontein and the poet)

(b)

Lady Anne alone at the Castle

it is midnight and pewter
outside   from the balcony
the stained gardens breathe
around me   I hear the garrison
and lust after you
already two weeks since you left
at the Imari basin
I imagine you shaving
from behind I burrow into the softer

tack   how robust the seam how virulently
your shirt swells out glides from
ashamed am I of my desire: to grab you by the hips
from behind   grow male
not to ride a broomstick but
to bloody fuck you between tincool buttocks into phenomenon

(c)
Cape of Good Hope

computerised city –
programmed underground
fine figured
power goes its terrible way

from your cybernetic memory
I want to take back my life
and my honour
and my name
all of it destroyed by the times we live in   hear me

out: I refuse to witness any longer
I refuse your decoding of freedom
I want to take my life back from you

as well: who does this word serve
how do I understand myself in this text-tortured land
how untouched do I hover

the freedom has already been won
in word and grenade
it has been taken   I
hear the sound of a thousand footfalls
oh do not ever pass me by

(d)
"I think I am the first" – Lady Anne on Table Mountain

you cannot paint it   colour will fail
the walking into waterfalls ragging
from ravine and stone   around us
the mountain paws the ground and rushes softly
in the mist   everything is held safely
by name
go
please go
why wait   so tiny suddenly
our figures in the gritty trench of words

but your feet beloved mountaineer
in tomato red socks and climbing boots
move peacefully from stone to stone
to my myopic eyes the mist becomes wiry
our two figures pegged against the rock face
where only damp sweeps between stone and cheek
stained with heather wherever my hands touch
and proteas hang like rucksacks of birds
– colour scrambles ziplike

the climb wipes out
everything between us
we become part of the slippery tongue-talking mountain
my blood pulses thinner than thin
as we go higher and higher
your secure footstep always in front of me
skullwet rain along our hot throats

from Platteklip ridge the wind bores
down on everything which is small and settler

more dense the route – naked
the abyss forces us closer
how do I preserve this memory my fellow poet of beauty
because see: everything is destructible
except the tongue against which we stretch
so small   the soft douche of the sea far below
you turn with the colour of your eyes smudged
                              and lonelier   yes
in your mouth lies the unbearable intimacy of consonance

from above you can really sketch everything
corruption seems only malicious   injustice temporary
and at its worst the dorpie below merely shoddy
see how cute the stonepoint castle   (my pretty abode!)
oh my God do we have to? we sing: save George our King

the wet clothes in front of the fire
compel us to break through layers of isolation
how do I bring this rainblind trip into words?
new words for survival
without destroying the breathless costliness
of sheltering each other   both knowing
how mercilessly it destroys this life between   to write

(e)
Lady Anne at Genadendal
10 May 1798

The three Moravian brothers housed us.
Late that afternoon the bell rings
through the valley
(to be heard as far as Stellenbosch).
Biduur.
We sit shyly
face to face with a hundred and fifty others.

My coat is wrinkled, I realise, they are clothed in skin,
the clay floor of the small church lies
languidly cut under reed carpets in afternoon sunlight.
My coat stays with me. I can smell them. They also me.
                                    The missionary
lifts his voice and says simply: mijn lieve vrienden.

But suddenly in this simplicity I notice Him –
quiet like a shiny bubble in my brain. Before Him
we are all naked but I see, as always, He sides with them:
the hungry, the poor, the crowds without hope,
the silent stubble, those without rights.
He becomes human in this building and turns to look at me.

It is good that I am here, it is good.
I remember my own church – the velvet matrix
with stones and corrupt chattering and I feel
God, how far away from You am I? How narrowly I know
still only myself – tired of white coinage
and they? The brushers of wigs,
the polishers of silver, the whitewashers of walls –
they know apart from themselves also my innermost bed.
God what do I do? How do I get rid
of this exclusive stain? Unexpectedly a song
swells into a garish passionate grief
supreme in pain (for the past or what is still to come?).

I sit surrendered in liturgical darkness,
my wrists frayed, my lips bleeding densely,
my head hangs in the softest sweat.
Before the closing prayer the missionary folds his hands
relentlessly into the eye of a needle.

I cut the ham into thin fragrant bundles
which the missionaries eat greedily,
swiping their forks through mustard.
"This you have to taste my brother!"
Our Madeira wine runs festively into cups.
I don't hear it. I don't see it.
Outside the moon grates herself insanely on the mountains.

More than millions tonight are huddling close to fires, crude
　　　　　　　　　　　　　　　　　　bread and beer,
songs, stories drifting from the coals.
How do I give up this snug cavity into which I was born?
Turn. Give. And my overstuffed soul? Isn't it simply looking
for something new to thrill about? Shouldn't every settler
carry his bundle of gold and decompose in regret and guilt –

even the choice stinks of privilege.
While the night is still lying in the valley
blood bursts on the peaks. I get up. Brushes, inks,
water. I drink some coffee, bread, cold meat,
my fingers clumsy with my coat. Along the footpath
my eyes scout for heights. Quickly stretch pages, mix greens, yes

green is the colour of balance, green endures
all colours, green is constantly broken
to absorb closer and further.
Black is only a shade of the deepest green.
In water-colour white is forbidden; dimension
comes from exclusion.

I have to find a framework for the complete landscape
if I want to survive my emotion. Try. Pitch the valley
into perspective, the rest will follow by itself.
But the missionary moves between me and the sun,
Gaspar the slave holds the umbrella.
I wave him impatiently out of the way,
but it's too late –
the fixed sun bursts brutally from above
and drums Genadendal into mirage.

I don't get it on paper. It doesn't fit,
the scale is wrong. I aim. I start afresh.
I stare until it dawns on me:
my pages will always spell window, spell distance,
the angle of incidence is always passive
and this is the way Madame wants to live
in this country: safely through glass,
wrapped in pretty pictures and rhymes
but I could
do
differently.
I could slowly pull back my hand and pick up a stone.

     I could throw it,
     shatter the glass
     to gasp, to thaw retchingly in this hip-high landscape
     at last.

(f)
Lady Anne looking out on the bay

A new ship arrived.
I prepare parcels and letters
(the coming and going of ships)
"latest" newspapers
– the written word the only harbour
for the travelling heart.

Then the smell hits us – unearthly,
so putrid it seems the most primordial
of all stenches. It's coming from the bay
says the cook. By midday everybody knows:
a slave ship is unlawfully looking to put to land
609 Congolese – my husband suspects
the hold is under water, a few have drowned; rice, nuts,
manioc finished. The obviously greedy upstart

captain of the ship implies that Governor Younge planned it all,
while he apparently hissed, "Did you have to hang
this maggots' nest for all and sundry of the Cape to see?"
"But why does it smell so?" "Annie, in the ship,"
my stolid husband, "they are lying row upon row –
packed shackled into filthy strings shelf upon shelf,
the doctor does not dare go down because of diarrhoea,
heat, stench; the deck deadly slippery from mucus and blood."

I turn the dessert spoon over and over –
silver, expensively heavy and catch myself
for days staring from every window
at the doomed ship in the bay.

At dusk a lament drifts towards the Castle,
a kind of howl, sobbing
from the abdomen of that pleading cargo of misery.
Through my telescope I see on the deck
shackled groups swaying to and fro in a macabre treaty
against death – a shoal of fins circling the ship
waiting for the stiff tussle of bodies
cut loose every morning and thrown overboard.

After I had seen that
'for many days my brain rushed forth
with a dim undetermined sense
of unknown modes of suffering
in my thoughts was a darkness
call it solitude
a blank desertion
no familiar shapes of trees
of sea or sky, no colours of green fields
but huge and mighty forms that do not live
like living men moved slowly through my mind
rotated my soul
penetrated walls'
haunting
haunting

(g)
Lady Anne as guide

I wanted to live a second life through you
Lady Anne Barnard – show it is possible
to hone the truth by pen
to live an honourable life in an era of horror

but from your letters you emerge
hand on the hip talented but a frivolous fool, pen
in sly ink, snob, naive liberal
being spoilt from your principles by your useless husband
you never had real pluck
            now that your whole frivolous life has arrived
            on my desk, I go berserk: as a metaphor, my Lady,
                        you're not worth a fuck

(h)
my dear Dundas

thus begins your new governor:
commission on every slave ship illegally dropping anchor
the following "free blacks" were executed this morning
for being "rebellious"

Domingo of Bengale
Moses Aaron of Makassar
Joost Ventura
Sampoernaij Abraham de Vyf
Rebe of Guinee
Jan Coridon
Mira Moor
Kijaija Moeda
and Claas Claasz of Bengale

just a list of heretics
for future composers
they hang this morning
on the open ground
next to the Castle
a decorative marimba

Lady Anne leaves the Cape

Andrew follows me with dog eyes. Why don't we talk!
I am so aware of my wrinkles, my stained hands,
I am really so much older than him – but he seems
to want to say sorry, or, nothing has changed between us
or, I am the best you could get
while you are all that I ever wanted.
The ship sent word: I have to board at noon –
loss suddenly has a clear thread.

A few Dutch friends wait on the beach.
I turn to the mountain: May God protect this land
from sorrow, may it never be destroyed by what freedom demands.
We row to the ship in a flat boat.
On the ship I wait at the rails while moving away
from me under salute is: everything, becoming smaller: the marrow
of slavery, tyranny, ignorance, beauty and terror in suspense,
a continent of promises, contours of soul so ultimately generous.

It is dark
with small light pools of lanterns
the ship shuffles away into the night.

(j)
you are being remembered for your parties Lady Anne

daughter of the House of Lindsay
heroine with the thousand faces
this poem is our final showdown

woman for whom I've sharpened my blade for so many years

naked (without possessions) next to your so-called pool
toe-nails yellowish beautiful calves (brutally
I stare) sagging knees the skin of your thighs

is old apple

your rusty breasts (in paintings
grotesquely bound) have areola and nipple
in one soft point because of no breastfeeding

(despite your drawing of the breastfeeding woman)

your weak abdomen I gather in my hand
it dissolves rennet-like into your fit vagina
gluey this big cream-coloured oyster

how close I am to you my inhibitions set me free

nothing missing in this brief assault
except that you have become beautiful
to me and movingly brave

my head turns to search for your sound in the Castle

my cheek I hold against the dogroses
the steps the water   like a wild shoot
your delicate nose blooms in a showcase downstairs

I bend to touch you overcome with tenderness

your barren hands rattle like reeds
you treated us always like an interesting park

but I look into your thin eyes
sparring blue even here next to your bath
only one life we have

in which we want to be loved forever

not opposite but together in this verse
lightfoot and without qualms the water takes you
into its lap I want to hold you God I've become attached to your

soapy elbows with crayons in clever perspective

your neck stylishly turned somewhat bohemian
in the blond shavings of your hair
upset I mourn beloved friend

your complete radiant uselessness

(k)
Andrew Barnard at the Cape to Lady Anne in London

I shudder
when I think
of the distance
between us.
Pray for me
love
as I always do
for you.

I will write
to my Anne
when I get back
from the hinterland.
May the Almighty
keep her
as always.

(l)
Lady Anne in Wimpole

the chestnut trees in pots
my hands dirty
when the message came

(but I had a letter yesterday!)
how can it be

how can it be
that that day passed over me
just like any other day?
that I sleep have tea
laugh and potter
while half of me
is already dead?

(m)
Lady Anne got back

your slave brought me
a handful of relics:

– a locket with my hair
– a green purse I knitted for you
– your medicine

of fever says Pawell
near Stellenbosch

the doctor from the Cape was too late
there was no one with you

you are buried on the road to Green Point
a small funeral
and wind from the sea

(n)

neither family nor friends says Lady Anne

tonight everything speaks through the dead
      towards me
your brittle bundle of bones
my longestloved beloved
lies lonely and longingly cradled somewhere lost
and lean
I am overwhelmingly awake tonight
of me so little has become
you are all I had in this world
beloved deathling
alone and cold it is behind my ribs
Africa had me giving up all
it is so dark
it is so bleak
soft beloved taunter
of me so little has become
I am down
to my last skin

Six
The house of sweets

how long

how long do we mean to last here?
we who have been wrecked against this lush continent
without ever indisputably landing in Africa
we in our American Colonial style houses
surrounded by parks and gardens
to escape the claim of the landscape
we who walk on kelims, talk in a Dutch dialect
listen to German lieder and read English poetry
who eat bacon and eggs for breakfast
hang out in western fashions
fly north past the continent for holidays
to drown in music and art galleries in our countries of origin
back home under Domsaitis's Prussian paintings
seek consolation with Islay Malt in Finnish glass

why not? here we are after three centuries nothing more
than pieces of western curiosa

our half a town

(a)

Lategansingel

you have a mistress
you walk you caress
as if somebody else
sings within you

your consideration towards me is painful
you want to convince yourself
that you have only been good to me

at the seaside I tried to yearn you back
by pretending that for myself I am enough
with sun and water you washed off me
could not hold onto my slippery body my thick hair

one night on the beach
my tongue was casting deep into the waves
to fable your blinding body
back into my arms

coolly you raced me
back to the flat
went to buy cigarettes
I saw you making a call from the booth

you cannot point a finger at anything
like shells I arrange our children
nowhere a space should open up
to force you to say the words

amused you watch us
objectively you make your calculations
and nothing that I do or am
seems suddenly enough reason to stay

at home during the day
I limp about with my useless wet body
find dead scales
between the sheets

every morning when you say goodbye
I smell you and withhold my hands modestly
from your lips – to fold them afterwards
behind the closed front door

around my diaphragm of fear

(b)

half undressed we stand
on each side of the cream-coloured bed
barefoot on plush pile carpets
screaming at each other

my seersucker dungaree slips onto its coat hanger
your shoes fall into the cupboard turned inwards
you humiliate me in front of others! your testes peel
from your tightfit briefs into pyjamas

how else to silence your unbearable arrogance?
you ask   I turn away from the cupboard and do not say:
you, my dear husband, I can cleave with a few sentences
spill your intestines like lightning on the coffee table

dry my hands
on a few punctuation marks
leave the party and you
to suckle consolation on your own

what prevents me? what makes me utter
the most infantile phrases   light accusations
bouncing blandly off your salacious body
what makes me cry in strange surroundings

that in the mirror I cannot endure myself
fold my arm protectively over my breast
where freely swinging clothed in steam
two rancorous wounds rage?

              (c)

absent-minded across the table
the lovely wife of an honest man
plays with two grains of rice: round and round
the plate she taps them with her nail

the good man sighs:
she is so pretty!
each day he slips his arm around
her thin white back

he thinks how his nose nuzzles against
her freezing throat: how he melts
the ice in her mouth while his hands
pull the skirt from her legs

but at each meal she sits
absent-minded across the table
pushing two grains of rice
with her nail across the plate

at dark another takes her
he remembers
watching her till midnight
through half-closed lashes, how

her body rocked in lamentation, how
her hands snatched at each other
jumping from the bed, she screamed
but made no sound in the night

then through the streets
the barking dogs, he trailed her, gliding
to the cemetery, and saw her scoop
soil from the nearest grave:

to have the corpse, to scrape
at the rotted flesh with her nails
to gorge that meat like porridge, piece
by piece, to lick the cadaver clean

absent-minded, across the table
the lovely wife of an honest man
plays with two grains of rice, thoughtfully
she taps them   round and round her plate

(translated by Patrick Cullinan)

(d)

Mondays the farmers come to town
with bakkies spattered in mud
to drop rosy-cheeked children at the hostel
and take mail, spare parts and co-op mealie meal back to the farm

in the mornings when they open their barns
forty angels appear
ten with tractors at their heads
ten with combine harvesters at their feet

ten who wake
ten who brake
around them rises
some earthly paradise

Wednesdays the town ladies have tea
dieted to the collarbone
in three-piece pastel suits
they gather around the yellowwood table knowing: the tea

will be poured Mary Mary from the silver pot
into hey diddle diddle Royal Albert
cups which tinkle and wee, wee, wee a porcelain dove
comes all the way home on the crocheted table cloth

the children play outside: Marli, Carli, naughty girl
turns the sprinkler on Lize and Rize   Cornel and Marisan
(or Marizaan or Mari-Zane) rollerblade with Jacques, Malan
and Jean-Herman in the shady street

on Fridays the ladies from the farms have their hair done
fat little stock doves fluff from German cars
parked bumper to bumper down the main street
in the back waits Liesbet with the youngest heir

laugh baby laugh
your father went a-hunting
with a telescopic Sauer and Sohn 30.08

hickory dickory dock read the city hall's clock
plump white fingers are protruding from the cage
and outside the house of sweets
hands are stoking a true fire of rage

demonstration lecture

Mo. Morning 3rd period 9h30 room A29
lecturer: Mrs A. Samuel   subject: Afrikaans Spec.SOD 1A
theme: plurals   dream dreams   drum drums

outside a sudden noise
as reams of schoolchildren
contour down the hill to assemble shouting
at the college gates   "Riots, Miss," says Basil calmly

through the window I look down at them: like columns
of ants the children cling to the fences
as if in a dream I walk down the stairs

hear stones hitting my white car
with drumthin snaps of tin
when the front window breaks into foam
a roar rises from the crowd

a tremor moves through my heart
students run from classrooms
hurl slogans   personnel ordered to the staff room
police on their way

I, who fear nothing
stand totally numb
filled with the icy terror of being unknown
wall-less white and hated

police stop in coverings of steel
flasks of teargas thick grey guns
over their shoulders bullets stream
like strings of copper beads

radio orders   barbed wire
in the casspirs I see the faceless outline
of each marksman a child's body
is loaded onto a jeep to bleed or die between boots

under escort we leave the bushes of smoke
breaking windows and the township where flames
break out like cannas on dark stems

on the other side
of the barricade
my chalk-white husband
waits

class boycotts bus boycotts
nervous next to each other lie town
and other town   impenetrable casspirs
roam the dark smoking streets

where black used to roll out daily the background
for white to move conspicuously
whites now slink bewildered from door to stoep
to shop in the desolate centre of town

muffled in locked houses we discuss:
why such a terror of schoolkids
who cannot be armed with anything more
than stones and dreams?

but we know
with the best and toughest wood revolution is being built
the artery is young
and the hand sparking the fire is the hand
which will
ultimately snap dream to drum

Jerusalemtrekkers

(a)

daily we live the transition
from smog corrugated iron
from crowded winding roads
township (of which some know

only the outline) to the inside rooms
of the owners   Mohaung wa hao –
your mercy – mme re tsamaye
ka pelo tse ntle tse hlwekileng

your ears are filled with our songs
at the fringes scratch the snow white chorales
by which name
do we summon dreams

other than the obsolete name of God?
You who simultaneously liberate and oppress
what is it in the word white?
what gives it a better sound than black?

say it: both lie equally on the tongue
from which meat do whites grow so high?
oh the guts to be
not windbag or jackal

but mighty tree growing into one's black self
corruption comes from the shielding
of guilt behind violence   suffering then becomes

an end a god unto itself
but liberatory suffering brings
the season of liberation   forefather our
black blood demands: a redistribution of pain

     (b)

we are committed to being involved
we pray for a mighty riot
we fear neither failure nor violence
nor death our family strangles us

for a vision   we pay the pleading
price daily we trek to the point
be it only an end
disgraceful among blackjack and povertybush

be it a fever to somehow live something
as a winged human being to see some sense
in it all   to hear things fall into place
after a single whipcrack

the further back the horizon
the more difficult to imagine
the more bitter the memory –
oh City, framework of all movement

City that is always heart
I see you in front of me shining
stripped of god and jesus
aimed-for City
which is at last humane and soul

Country of grief and grace

(a)

between you and me
how desperately
how it aches
how desperately it aches between you and me

so much hurt for truth
so much destruction
so little left for survival

where do we go from here

your voice slung
in anger
over the solid cold length of our past

how long does it take
for a voice
to reach another

in this country held bleeding between us

(b) .

in the beginning is seeing
seeing for ages
filling the head with ash
no air
no tendril
now to seeing speaking is added
and the eye plunges into the wounds of anger

seizing the surge of language by its soft bare skull
hear oh hear
the voices all the voices of the land
all baptised in syllables of blood and belonging
this country belongs to the voices of those who live in it
this landscape lies at the feet at last
of the stories of saffron and amber
angel hair and barbs
dew and hay and hurt

(c)

speechless I stand
whence will words now come?
for us the doers
the hesitant
we who hang quivering and ill
from this soundless space of an Afrikaner past?
what does one say?
what the hell does one do
with this load of decrowned skeletons origins shame and ash
the country of my conscience
is disappearing forever like a sheet in the dark

(d)

we carry death
in a thousand cleaving spectres
affected
afflicted
we carry death

it latches its mouth to our heart
it sucks groaningly
how averse lures the light on our skin
it knows
our people carry death
it resembles ourselves
our stomachs wash black with it
a pouch of ink
we carry death into the houses
and a language without mercy
suddenly everything smells of violence

death snaps its repentless valves in our language
yes, indefatigable meticulous death

      (e)

deepest heart of my heart
heart that can only come from this soil
brave
with its teeth firmly in the jugular of the only truth that matters
and that heart is black
I belong to that blinding black African heart
my throat bloats with tears
my pen falls to the floor
I blubber behind my hand
for one brief shimmering moment this country
this country is also truly mine

and my heart is on its feet

(f)

because of you
this country no longer lies
between us but within

it breathes becalmed
after being wounded
in its wondrous throat

in the cradle of my skull
it sings   it ignites
my tongue   my inner ear   the cavity of heart
shudders towards the outline
new in soft intimate clicks and gutturals

I am changed for ever   I want to say
forgive me
forgive me
forgive me

you whom I have wronged, please
take me

with you

(g)

this body bereft
this blind tortured throat

the price of this country of death
is the size of a heart

grief comes so lonely
as the voices of the anguished drown on the wind

you do not lie down
you open up a pathway with slow sad steps
you cut me loose

into light — lovelier, lighter and braver than song
may I hold you my sister
in this warm fragile unfolding of the word humane

(h)

what does one do with the old
which already robustly stinks with the new
the old virus slyly manning the newly installed valves
how does one recognise the old
        with its racism and slime
its unchanging possessive pronoun
what is the past tense of the word hate
what is the symptom of brutalised blood
of pain that did not want to become language
of pain that could not become language

what does one do with the old
how do you become yourself among others
how do you become whole
how do you get released into understanding
how do you make good
how do you cut clean
how close can the tongue tilt to tenderness
or the cheek to forgiveness?

a moment
a line which says: from this point onwards
        it is going to sound differently
because all our words lie next to one another on the table now
shivering in the colour of human
we know each other well
each other's scalp and smell   each other's blood
we know the deepest sound of each other's kidneys in the night
we are slowly each other
anew
new
and here it starts

        (i)

(but if the old is not guilty
does not confess
then of course the new can also not not be guilty
nor be held accountable
if it repeats the old

things may then continue as before
but in a different shade)

In transit – a cycle of the early nineties

(a)

first christmas weekend under the state of emergency 1988

we murmur on the verandah at dusk
it's as if ears stir in the ivy
strung in blood around the house and fences
unexpected forms wait in the shade
we hesitate
opened letters fall into the house
someone runs up the street
we wait
the garden rustles in mists of suspicion
we speak more softly
so many children in prison
so many arrests
the trains moan restlessly
is it true
so many thousands of children?
rumours crawl from the foundations like rats

christmas cookies ginger beer a little tree
children play with cousins
the turkey hisses stuffed with tarragon thyme and raisins
under bows of light families bob in boats
the river slushes against the keels
crackers crack
black workers at the mooring place look up
unfathomably

I play the piano my children dressed
as Mary and Joseph and angel sing:
away in a manger
a trough for his bed

(translated by Karen Press)

(b)
refused march at kroonstad monday 23 october 1989

my thirty-seventh year to heaven
I wake up in my town that I can only
experience as backward in flat air-conditioned
little shops jails with rose streamers
fluttering fragrance
the house embraced by a scorching wind on this day
the day of my birthday while thousands
start crowding close
on the small greened square between town
and township: the march through my town today

ten I asked for   perhaps we'll find ten
ten whites who want to see the town reconciled the way it
wants to spread its own freedom over cool
banks   crickets carve the midday
bare and willows smell
like bark   for the sake of ten of eight don't be angry
for the sake of five, alright then, of three for the sake
of three don't destroy
the town   sulphur and fire
hold back so that we can occupy it over again, new

roses gasp salmon-tongued from their buds at tea delicate
sandwiches light murmuring of peace
      spoilt gifts heartfelt wishes
            I know the march should now be heading to the left
            as far as the main street
here I sit with everything white – thus I fail completely   my tongue
                                                              too thin
my writing too gasping my language uncertain
      in hand and flees
                  to paper   purblind town and all that burns
is my fist beside my own salt pillar of fear

(translated by Karen Press)

(c)
Brentpark March 1990

how to write this land
how to say it arm in arm   row upon row
fluttering in front our minister's coat
the steel wall
yellow casspirs
bandoliers with fingerthick bullets
a slit-eyed policeman let the chain slip
the alsatian yaws up to my face as if possessed
cold soots the wind

my heart tolls heavy and dull like a decomposing pear
on the casspir a man from my neighbourhood
his teeth gnarling venom from his lips
you disgrace whites
another kicks open the door of the police van
and curses all kaffirfuckers

slowly the procession
our first march   in silence
from the little bridge on the fringe of the coloured area
we have been allowed to march a meagre five metres
a landscape completely stops breathing
we stand up   we stand together
we clasp arms   we hear a strength flowing from us
see:
we march therefore we are

bullets crack   violent assaulting sounds
lightfooted we sow in all directions
hide in unknown backyards slink along fences
get one by one back to the scene of the crime
everybody tells his eyes
we laugh and shudder
we touch one another again and again

a march with a hundred eyes has scorched us a new skin

(d)
1992

stones against the corrugated iron
a window bursts inward

automatically I wipe the splinters from the table
take an empty page   sharpen my pencil
let the shavings fall god knows neatly into a tissue
instinctively I begin writing
another round of shards
children yell   someone's hand is bleeding
another window and another ...
Darrel runs past me – a dagger in his hand
his eyes glitter as if from somewhere else
the boys in the class pull from their pockets:
penknives, daggers, bottlenecks, screwdrivers
something burns   somebody shrieks rhythmically
against the door frame a pupil is pushed
a knife protruding next to his balls
a blot bleeds on his threadbare pants
a window smashes in my face
I dive down under my table – pencil in hand
I'm dying for a cigarette is jesus the only thought in my head

if a stone hits me I'll
just simply die
anyway already starving from the violation of space
of property of privacy of life
on ridges where nobody's life has any worth

under the table I try to get hold of the word
a single word enabling me from this side to transgress

decades of death in the valleys
where white families disintegrate – overweight
and bewildered they sit deeper into their houses
bullying thicklegged sons at loggerheads
in front of the tv timorous daughters take to their heels
wives wrinkle moist in frills
while the patriarch coughs on the toilet

behind the broken border fences
chicken pens rust among khakibush and weed
next to crumbling troughs devil thorns lie lush
telephone poles tumble on fallow fields
nobody's eyes feel the borders down any more

under the searing heat of the hardboard ceiling
on fake leather sofas their fingers lock around ice cold beer
fuck the kaffirs
has finally changed into
the fucking kaffirs

(f)
1995

I say it beforehand
loud
I stand for nothing
I join ranks with nowhere
nobody comes near me

all of them look the same
all are men all
are necks all
pods of power

the generals and brigadiers and ministers
and headmen-generals sit cuddling their cocks
plaiting their penises
trashing a whole country with the alternating faeces
of politics and violence
all are sly
all feel fuckall

Lord from whence cometh our salvation?
in the corridors lie money and glass
stop streets of meat
taxis become gargoyles of blood
and everybody wants to have
and everybody wants to keep

between nobody nothing nowhere gets healed
between nowhere and nobody nothing survives
nobody offers nothing
nothing
       vapour
nothing
      balming
nothing   something
     healing
something gentle
nothing mildly human

I say it beforehand
I stand for nothing
I join ranks with no one

I repugn completely

SEVEN
LIVING THE LANDSCAPE

a one-dimensional song for the northern free state, more specifically middenspruit

most beloved state of heart estranged from spring
where maize crackles like stars
with rustblond beards distilling the moonlight
where sunflower fields spread handkerchiefs in the valleys
where clouds roll like horses
the late sun shoots out peacock feathers
across plump and broody fluff-green hills
each farm dam windmilled with willows
evening's last sparks fizzling
through heron-still waters

most beloved state of heart estranged from spring
where tràins with ferns of smoke
go easily clicking and clucking each winter
over redgrass flecked with sparrow wings
over khakibush and blackjack echoing ironstone and guineafowl
reedbrown sandstonebrown dassiebrown winterbrown
white leghorn tufts in marshes
where partridges wobble like vetkoek at twilight
every winter morning cracks apart sharp as needles
a crisp willow-whip splits the frost
       the far-off puff of dung fires
       autumn feeding only on poplars
power-lines chattering softly to each other

most beloved flatlands of my heart
where the jack-knife of winter
casts itself completely
into the green harvest of summer
so many years I've tried to deaden our tie
and make your plains fertile in some other way
but each season I come to trace you again and again
for if I die this way I die
even in boland and bushveld
month in month out your redgrass blossoms in my eyes

red grass

a swish of redgrass as far as the eye can leak
I crawl through the wire like someone seduced – heart in the throat –
and it sings silklike it sings redgrass stems into the sky
strutting seedpods in rust and tawny
little grasshoppers splutter
and it rustles   it lisps in ankledeep shrub
it crackles silk and feeler signals
lightfooted to that side
a redgrasspath a redgrasslightfootpath's halfbody fragrance
at ground level sprouting tiny roots
breathing I stand human in the first clump erect

I adore *Themeda triandra* the way other people adore God

christmas 1992

after the rains
the veld gives herself like a slut to the green

of barren plains there is suddenly nothing of

everything sprees   everything revels
green among thorn trees
the karee heaves a vastrap
the wild olive jitterbugs
and for christmas the catbush tiptoes small red berries

wait, oh wait
every afternoon the gingergreen kuil is filled out
by a benevolent boon of clouds – all vernacularly white

the excess of the veld is so unimpaired
so sudden
so cicada sung
so lavishly festive
and fraught with green
it attests to a bloody insensitivity towards us
us to whom the veld belongs
belied and belittled, betrayed we feel
we to whom the veld belongs
eroded bewildered assaulted we feel
we to whom the veld belongs

this is perhaps our last together
so like this

land

under orders from my ancestors you were occupied
had I language I could write for you were land my land

but me you never wanted
no matter how I stretched to lie down
in rustling blue gums
in cattle lowering horns into Diepvlei
rippling the quivering jowls drink
in silky tassels in dripping gum
in thorn trees that have slid down into emptiness

me you never wanted
me you could never endure
time and again you shook me off
you rolled me out
land, slowly I became nameless in my mouth

now you are fought over
negotiated divided paddocked sold stolen mortgaged
I want to go underground with you land
land that would not have me
land that never belonged to me

land that I love more fruitlessly than before

(translated by Karen Press)

four summer poems for Cape Town

(a)

the bay blinks milk
sailboats sown like duwweltjies
behind wax paper the mountain gnashes from the blue

(b)

the lion stares at the mountain
fondle the reef of small trees
cuddle the stony back of the head
put your hand on the downy flank – for quite some time
until she flabbily shakes her head
and gets up
see! houses and flats slip down the slopes
and turns her thighs to the north
shake-paw she walks along the waves
searching
for something humanless
like a desert

(c)

come day! come mountain
bloused in blue
come make me yours
gather me against yourself
lightsoft bundles
of bluebreast sky
fathoms and fathoms thereof

(d)

is it wide here
wider than the widest of water and wind
is it soft here
is it green here
and always blue
am I without name here

in me inflamed am I with love
for so lovely

paternoster

I stand on a massive rock in the sea at Paternoster
the sea beats strips of light green foam
      into the air

fearless
I stare down every bloody damn wave
in the gut as it breaks
the rock quakes under my soles
my upper leg muscles bulge
my pelvis casts out its acquired resigned tilt

like hell! I am rock I am stone I am dune

distinct my tits hiss a copper kettle sound
my hands clasp Moordbaai and Bekbaai
my arms tear ecstatically past my head:
I am
I am
god hears me
a free fucking woman

GLOSSARY

bakkies:	small pick-up trucks
Bekbaai:	Mouth Bay
biduur:	prayer meeting
boland:	mountainous area in the south-western region of the Western Cape province, South Africa
bushveld:	areas of South Africa's northern provinces with bushy, often thorny, vegetation
casspirs:	armoured troop carriers
dassie:	hyrax
Diepvlei:	deep pan or marsh
Domsaitis:	Prussian-born painter who lived in South Africa for 16 years
dorpie:	small town
duwweltjies:	small thorns
Genadendal:	mission station in Western Cape province, South Africa
kapater:	castrate

middenspruit: name of farm in Free State province of
South Africa where the poet was born

mijn lieve vrienden: (*Dutch*) my dear friends

Mohaung wa hao ...
mme re tsamaye
ka pelo tse ntle
tse hlwekileng: (*Sesotho*) Your mercy is enough ... we walk
with kind and forward-looking hearts

Moordbaai: Murder Bay

Pawell: male servant of Lady Anne Barnard's husband

Platteklip: a gorge on Table Mountain, Cape Town

sommer: just (*adv.*)

spaza: informal shop in (usually) black residential areas

vastrap: fast dance popular in certain boer communities

verkramp: ultra conservative

vetkoek: fried dumpling